Ancient Moorish (Black) History Revealed: Chit-Chats & Comments off the Web Vol. VI

Ayannah Makiidah Taylor

Copyright © 2012 Author Name

All rights reserved.

ISBN: -13:
978-1479338764

ISBN-10:
1479338761

DEDICATION

This Book is Dedicated to my mother Janis L Williams and Grandparents Walter and Lorraine Williams and teachers Mr. Scrudato and Mr. Roth.

CONTENTS

Acknowledgment i

1. Chapter 5 (May 7th, 2012)

ACKNOWLEDGMENTS

I will like to acknowledge that if it wasn't for Dr. Malachi Z York I wouldn't know much as I know now. I hope he will be free soon from the kangaroo court that convicted him. I, Ayannah Taylor would like to thank my mother (Janis L Williams) and grandparents (Lorraine and Walter Sr. Williams) who had love for ourstory in particular "Moorish" as defined and researched by Cheikh Anta Diop, Gerald Massey and David MacRitchie and its original meaning of "Passionate love, of the sea, dark brown" - (not the modern meaning of the "predominantly Muslim/Hebrew Moors" of West Africa who recivilized Spain and Portugal). What people call "Black History," has been downplayed where the point, most Moors or blacks in the United States and Western Hemisphere think our story began with mass enslavement of Moors and that is totally unacceptable. I was 1st exposed by viewing one of the most beautiful golden pieces ever - King Tutankhamen's Funerary mask! I was hooked, lined and sinkered! From then on, others have inspired me or had taught me and given me education through private and public schools such as Dr. Malachi Z K. York, and the adults like Sitt Nafiysa, Sitt Faatima Senousi, Sayyid Mahwuwd, Sid Yuwsuf, Umm Samiyra, Umm Baaqiya, Umm Layaa (Sandra Fraser), 'Abdul Ali (Jerry Miller), Mr. J. A Rogers, Mama Zogbe, Cheikh Anta Diop, Gerald Massey, Sir Higgins, David MacRitchie. I also want to thank everyone who loves to learn and especially the people on Facebook as sis Naja Njoku and brothers Karaam Ellis and Dan Djudah Khemhai who have taught me things as well, and who keep pushing me to help educate others.

1) A Moorish/African Chief/King or Obi of Nnewi, Nigeria- Africa. Mongolia's imperial clothing is very similar to his garb and hat. Golden object in his hand matches the fine clothing!

Nnewi sounds a whole lot like the Assyrian city Nineveh. Nineveh (English pronunciation: /ˈnɪn.ɪv.ə/; Akkadian: Ninwe; Classical Syriac: ܢܝܼܢܘܹܐ; Hebrew: נינוה Nīnewē; Greek: Νινευη Nineuē; Latin: Nineve; Arabic: نينوى Naynuwa; Persian: نینوا Nainavā) was an ancient Assyrian city on the eastern bank of the Tigris River, and capital of the Neo Assyrian Empire. Its ruins are across the river from the modern-day major city of Mosul, in the Ninawa Governorate of Iraq.

The origin of the name Nineveh is obscure. Possibly it meant originally the seat of Ishtar, since Nina was one of the Babylonian names of that goddess. The ideogram means "house or place of fish," and was perhaps due to popular etymology (comp. Aramaic "nuna," denoting "fish").*

Rasheed: "The Aramaic for fish makes sense because in the Old Testament, Jonah was sent to speak against Nineveh in the belly of a "fish." That system must be in power now, given the "fish" symbolism of modern Christianity and especially Catholicism - namely is the headdress of the pope.

Ayannah Taylor: "Yes, thanks Rasheed Jamal for breaking that down. That is who is mostly against the Moors in this day and time the antithesis as Radu Cinnamar said in Transylvania Moonrise. They (Cat Holi ism) represent the male, while the Moors represent female! Very interesting! HMMM!

Rasheed: "Given the procession of ages and an influx of feminine energy, I think we all can see the effects from the spikes of these masculine and feminine energies being out of balance. One being overly dominant and the other suppressed. It's like shaking a hot bottle of soda or champagne. Contents under pressure."

Ayannah Taylor Thanks brother Rasheed. You are making much sense! Much love and respect.

Hubert: "I've read your discussion and as I have become enlightened, I noted also the fish shape of the golden emblem."

Rasheed: "The stories of Oannes come to mind when I think of fish symbolism. Also, the tales of Dagan, whom I believe were "fish headed" gods who were amphibious and came out of the water to teach the people about agriculture, science, mathematics, hunting, and architecture. The images of them show them wearing what seem to be wrist watches. As I type this, the reports of so called "unidentified flying objects" coming from underwater make sense if this "mythology" actually were to be verified historically since Mars' civilization was destroyed... And Venus is said to have had a far more dynamic past than what we know of. Yet, this may all be science fiction as far as these theories I've presented. It's interesting to see traces of validity left in the indigenous cultures of Africa and South America."

Rasheed: "The Pope actually represents Dagan in his dress... Though the Black Pope is actually in charge as far as we know. Yet, even then..."

Ayannah Taylor: "Oh Rasheed I just finished re reading this passage in Sibyls: The First Prophetess' of Mami Wata on page 14: "The first prophets of Mami Wata were African women. They were called Sibyls, meaning they were Mami Wata priestess and priests of the Oannes. Their prophecies are the oldest in the world. It is through the divine blood of these priestesses that the patriarchal kingships of the Pharaohs, and the Hebrew prophets and the Chaldean priests were born. It was the Sybil prophecy and magic that would later be imitated by a militant faction from these groups, who envious of her global positioning, rebelled against these divine matriarchal orders and seized their temples and overthrew their priestess hood as patriarchy began to dominate.""

Ayannah Taylor: "And you know Oannes is similar to pharaoh Unas/Unas or Oanes/Wenis. Then in Arabic Yuwnus (يوﻧس , Yūnus or يوﻧان, Yūnān) in Arabic meaning Jonah. and the 'aa' on Yunaan/Yunan represents two Jonahs."

Ayannah Taylor: "Rome was one of the major seats of these Moorish priestesses until they were finally exiled and support for them was crushed. They were persecuted and those catacombs in Rome are for them many whom were killed and family members had to sneak in and bring offerings and not the early Christians as often told."

Rasheed: "Wasn't Sybil or a variation of her mentioned by Daniel as a goddess of fortresses as well? And that linking to Jonah is indeed interesting... Where can I find that book? Seems like a missing link to the dispersion of Nile Valley Civilization.."

Ayannah Taylor: "Yes indeed Rasheed Jamal! On Google for the whole thing, but here is the mini version of the book link: http://books.google.com/books?id=ZTCpiKMiPk8C
The Sibyls: the First Prophetess' of Mami (Wata)
books.google.com."

Ayannah Taylor Oh and look on the ruler's right side a Dove or for some reason reminds me of a Sankofa bird.

Rasheed: "Is it a Sankofa bird, huh??"

Ayannah Taylor: "No, it is not. But for some reason it reminds me of one - just looking up instead of backwards."

Rasheed: "Its head and beak are made in the same shape... Maybe it's a variation. Or a sea gull?"

Ayannah Taylor: "Ok that is probably why the 1st thing that popped in my mind was a dove and I said kind of similar to the Sankofa bird. LOL"

Rasheed: "I agree. LOL"

A'aferti Khnum: "Powerful."

Ayannah Taylor: "Yes it is A'aferti Khnum."

Monique: "Wow, very Educational and Intriguing! Thank u!"

Ayannah Taylor: "You're welcome and thanks Monique."

2) King Esarhaddon who Esarhaddon (Akkadian: Aššur-ahhe-iddina "Ashur has given a brother to me"; Aramaic: ܐܣܪܚܕܘܢ ܐܣܪܚܕܢ; Hebrew: אֵסַר חַדֹּן];1] Greek: Ασαραδδων;[2] Latin: Asor Haddan[3]), was a king of Assyria who reigned 681 – 669 BC. He was the youngest son of Sennacherib and the Aramean queen Naqi'a (Zakitu), Sennacherib's second wife.

When, despite being the youngest son, he was named successor by his father, his elder brothers tried to discredit him. Oracles had named Esarhaddon as the person to free the exiles and rebuild Babylon, the destruction of which by Sennacherib was felt to be sacrilegious. Esarhaddon remained crown prince, but was forced into exile at an unknown place beyond Hanilgalbat (Mitanni), that is, beyond the Euphrates, most likely somewhere in what is now southeastern Turkey.

Sennacherib was murdered in 681 BC, some [who?] claim at the instigation of Esarhaddon, though this seems hardly likely, as he was not in a situation to exploit unrest arising from the death of his father. The biblical account is that his brothers killed their father after the failed attempt to capture Jerusalem and fled (2 Kings 19:37). He returned to the capital of Nineveh in forced marches and defeated his rival brothers in six weeks of civil war. He was formally declared king in spring of 681 BC. His brothers fled the land, and their followers and families were put to death. In the same year he began the rebuilding of Babylon, including the well-known Esagila and the Ekur at Nippur (structures sometimes identified with Tower of Babel).[4] The statues of the Babylonian gods were restored and returned to the city. In order not to appear too biased in favor of Babylonia, he ordered the reconstruction of the Assyrian sanctuary of Esharra in Ashur as well. Foreigners were forbidden to enter this temple. Both buildings were dedicated almost at the same date, in year two of his reign.*

Also, if you notice Esar is similar to Asar (Osiris) and Ha don is similar Adon or Adonai (אֲדֹנָי)- meaning (Master/Lord in Aramic/Hebrew).

Bossassi Bolia: "This was a Persian king right?"

Ayannah Taylor: "Close, but Assyrian Bossassi Bolia Kodia Tunde."

Corliss Lowery: "I love my history class on FB. Oops, u no our story."

Todd Teo: "Thanks for that.. Ayannah 1♥."

Ayannah Taylor: "LOL, Thanks Corliss! I'm glad you are learning and teach others too."

Kimoto: "His face is undeniably Negroid."

Ayannah Taylor: "Yes it is Kimota Ka and the late Michael Clark Duncan (the actor) looks like him from the side view. RIP!"

Queenstarletta: ♥"♥♥BLESSINGS. The curly/woolly hair and the shape of the nose give little room to doubt the ethnicity of this King.....!!! If this image is that of a Caucasian, then I'm the King of England..!!!"

 3) Actor Michael Clark Duncan started out as a bouncer than got lil acting gigs to making big movies. He has a really good resemblance to Assyrian King Esarhaddon without the beard. RIP Michael!

 4) The movie Centurion features JJ Field, Noel Clarke and Liam Cunningham; Macros, played by (Noel Clark- an English actor) is the strong, heroic Moorish/Black Roman. Of course they too started off as black and kept mixing and recruiting others to fight in their wars against other black and white tribes. This one was against the ancient Picts who were the original, indigenous Moors of Scotland.

 5) Nice pic! He looks like an actor on one of the Law shows on TV. Someone help me out!

6) Ghanaian Queen Mother from Mfantseman district, Ghana, Africa. I noticed whether the tribes are matrilineal or patrilineal they both have Queen Mothers.

7) Major Countries where Black Gold is King! These are the top 10 countries around the world with the most precious resources. As you can see in Africa, Libya (which was invaded and destroyed by Nato forces, and now foreign corps coming in like vultures and taking their stuff); Nigeria (fuel subsidies getting rough), now add Kenya (said to have more than Saudi Arabia) to the mix. Ghana also got some oil and gas as well.

8) What is happening with all the bleaching??? Where is the love Sammy Sosa? Too much Self Hate.

Nima: "Sad."

Ayannah Taylor: "Thanks Nima. Yes it is indeed sad, But he is only acting out all the self-hate he has been taught! SMH. I wonder can they reverse the procedure and he can get his melanin back?"

Nima Falconer: "I really hope this photo is photo shopped."

Ayannah Taylor: "Yes please be! But I somehow doubt that. He was photographed with his wife somewhere I'd seen like a month ago, looks like a ghost."

Nima: "Wow!!! So sad he was once very handsome. What he doesn't understand is God doesn't make any mistakes, but he did."

Ayannah Taylor: "Amen Nima!"

DaRuddest: "Perhaps it's not bleaching. Maybe he has a skin disorder."

Ayannah Taylor: "DaRuddest I think he admitted to bleaching, but called it skin cleansing or something like that."

DaRuddest: "SMH. Wt., was he cleaning skin molecules??? I f****** can't."

Ayannah Taylor: "LMBO! I have to find the article. Someone posted it a while back. SMH! Yes."

Ayannah Taylor: "Oh I'd found it here it is: http://sports.espn.go.com/mlb/news/story?id=4642952

Sosa: Facial cream caused lightening of skin
sports.espn.go.com
Speaking publicly for the first time since photos of him from a recent musical award ceremony were published on the Internet, Sammy Sosa said that the skin lightening is the result of the use of a facial cosmetic cream.

DaRuddest Jones: -_-

Ayannah Taylor: "Thanks brother Victor Muhammad for your tactful and on point input."

Ayannah Taylor And sisters too! Poisoned Mind now Poisoned Skin Omari Stayingaway.

King Omari: "THAT IZ ANOTHA FORM OF SELF MUTILATION..."

Ayannah Taylor: "Physically and Psychologically too!"

King Omari: "THAT IZ SO TRUE....HE IZ ALSO DENOUNCING HIZ PARENTZ AND HIZ CULTURE....."

Ayannah Taylor: "But because of his mind been poisoned to thinking white is right due to God and his Son being White then he and all others dark like him must be Bad. This goes back to the 50 years (and even most recently), - old experiment where the lady had given children two choices of a black child and white one and most of all the kids picked the white one for good and hardly none of the black kids picked their own."

King Omari: "YOU KNOW THAT IZ CORRECT, BUT IN THIZ DAY AND AGE OF ACCCELERATED INFORMATION HE SHOULD KNOW BETTER.....HE CHOOSES TO ALTER HIMSELF DO TO SELF HATE TO FIT IN A LIGHTER SHADE SOCIETY WHICH DOES'NT EXIST BUT HE TRICKS HIMSELF TO BELIEVING THAT IT DOES, WHEN IT ALL BOILZ DOWN HE IZ STILL WHAT HE IZ AND AFTER THEY USE HIM UP HE WILL FIND OUT!!!!!"

Rsinis Re : "He doesn't know he's black. They don't teach them that in Spanish speaking islands."

King Omari: "HE HAZ BEEN IN AMERICA LONG ENOUGH TO KNOW THAT, BUT HE CHOOSES NOT TO BELIEVE THAT BECAUSE HE WANTZ TO FIT IN A ONCE AGAIN "LIGHT SHADE SOCIETY."

King Omari: "HE WANTZ TO BE "WHITE," WHY ELSE HE WOULD BLEACH HIZ SKIN BRO BRO!?"

King Omari: "HE BLEACHED HIZ SKIN BECAUSE HE KNOWZ THAT HE IZ BLACK!"

Salina M: "He looks so bad!!!!!!!!"

9) Ancient Shark from millions of years ago still survives in the oceans. The **frilled shark** (*Chlamydoselachus anguineus*) is one of two extant species of shark in the family Chlamydoselachidae, with a wide but patchy distribution in the Atlantic and Pacific Oceans. This uncommon species is found over the outer continental shelf and upper continental slope, generally near the bottom though there is evidence of substantial upward movements. It has been caught as deep as 1,570 m (5,150 ft.), whereas in Suruga Bay, Japan it is most common at depths of 50–200 m (160–660 ft.). Exhibiting several "primitive" features, the frilled shark has often been termed a "living fossil". It reaches a length of 2 m (6.6 ft.) and has a dark brown, eel-like body with the dorsal, pelvic, and anal fins placed far back. Its common name comes from the frilly or fringed appearance of the gill slits, of which there are six pairs with the first pair meeting across the throat. *

Ayannah Taylor Shark anyone? LOL

10) Ancient Kushites/Egyptians live on thru their descendants all over Africa and the world. The ancient Egyptians comprised of such tribes as the Bantu- (South Africa), Akan- (West Africa), Ewe- (West Africa and East Africa, Ga, Wolof- (West and East Africa), Hamer- (East Africa, Tebu - (North and West Africa) etc. Follow the languages and you can clearly see the links.

AKAN

| **AKAN WORDS** | **MEANINGS** |

Muntu	To ask people to move out.
Khem	To divide or shout. Ancient Egyptian Khem black, up there from the female deity of the sky
Fanti is the	name of a large section of Akan people in the Central Region of Ghana.
Menu	Inside of me
Tutu	To uproot. Incidentally the founder of the Asante Empire is called Osei-TUTU. (Tutu is also South African) Bishop Tutu.
Tebu	The name of an Akan town in Ghana. Also a tribe of Moors in North and West Africa, Libya, Niger etc. Tebu is Akan for Taiba or Thebes – ancient Egypt.
Maati	I heard
Per-Me	to like me Per in French is for moi, meaning "me." Per is also ancient Egyptian for Great house/Pharaoh.
Anu in Akan	Mouth. Anu ancient Egyptian On for the city of the Sun.
Ati means	torn.

MERIOTIC (SUDANESE/EGYPTIAN) WORDS

MERIOTIC (Ancient Sudanese script)	English	BEJA (Modern Sudanese/Egyptian)
i	arrive at this point	bi 'went'
t	'he, she'	ta 'she'
ya	go	yak 'start'
rit	'look'	rhitaa 'you saw'
an(a)	plural suffix	aan 'these'
d(d)	say	di(y)
lb	energy, dynamic	liwa 'burn'
ken	to realize	kana 'to know'
bk	'ripen'	bishakwa 'to be ripe'

BANTU WORDS

BANTU WORDS	MEANINGS
BATU	Another name for Sudan or Bantu
Untu	UNTU - things (Ancient Egyptian and Bantu) men, women, people
MUNTU	Warrior God from Thebes (see Budge). Also see placed Temples Bantu Philosophy as well as Johanz' MUNTU for documentation that states MUNTU is not only the name for a human being but for GOD.
SIUA, SYUA,	The Sun. Ancient Egyptian Shu - god of the sky, day, sunlight
NAMA , INAMA, NYAMA	flesh, skin, meat. Ancient Egyptian INM
SHIKANA,	hold each other, embrace each other, be friends **In ancient Egyptian SHKN means same thing**
RERA	**To nurse a child, the same in ancient Egyptian RR to nurse a child.**

WOLOF

WOLOF/ANCIENT EGYTPIAN	MEANING
aam - aam	: seize (take this)
aar - aar	: paradise (divine protection)
Aku - Aku :	foreigners (Creole descendants of European traders and African wives)
anu - K.enou	: pillar
atef - ate	: a crown of Osiris, judge of the soul (to judge)
ba - bei	: the ram-god (goat)
bai - bai	: a priestly title (father)
ben ben - ben ben	: overflow, flood
bon - bon	: evil
bu - bu	: place
bu nafret - bu rafet	: good place
bu bon - bu bon	: evil place
da - da	: child
deg - deega	: to see, to look at carefully (to understand)
deresht - deret	: blood. Deshret is also Red Crown in ancient Egypt
diou - diou rom	: five

djit - djit	: magistrate (guide)

**

Ayannah Taylor: "Merci Beacoup OluKorede."
OluKorédé S.: "Ayannah Taylor, De rien ma soeur.!!!"

11) A picture named the "Maure" by Sir Christopher Wren (1632-1723). And No he is not an islamicized Moor either. He is Christian. If you all recall the pale European guy in the movie "The Black Knight," kept on calling Martin Lawrence, "Moor," this and Moor that and yes Martin the Moor/black Knight was "Christian!"

Le Maure (The Moor) Sir Christopher Wren - (1632-1723)

Maur, m. Fr. Lat. dark, 413
Maura, /. It. Ger. Lat. dark, 413
Maure,/. Fr. Lat. dark, 413
Maurice, m. Fr. Eng. Lat. Moorish, 415
Mauricio, m. Port. Span. Lat. Moorish
Maurids, m. Dan. Lat. Moorish, 415
Mauritius, m. Lat. Moor, 415
Maurits, m. Dutch, Lat. Moor, 415
Maurizio, m. Ital. Lat. Moor, 415
Mauro, m. Rom. Lat. Moor, 418
Maurus, m. Lat. Moor, 413
Meurisse, m. Fr. Lat. Moor, 414
Moric, m. Bohm. Slav. Lat. Moor, 415
Moricz, m. Hung. Lat. Moor, 415
Moritz, m. Dan. Lat. Moor, 415
Moritz, m. Ger. Lat. Moor, 415
Moriz, m. Ruts. Lat. Moor, 415
Morris, m. Ir. Lat. Moor,
Morgance, f. m. French, Kelt, sea dweller, ii. 156
Morgan, m. Welsh, Kelt, sea dweller, 418, ii. 156
Morgana, f. Eng. Kelt, sea dweller, ii.156
Morgue, f. Fr. Kelt, sea dweller, ii. 156

Morgwen, f. Welsh, Kelt, sea lady, ii. 156
Morgwn, m. Welsh, Kelt, sea dweller, ii
THE GENERAL HISTORY OF IRELAND by Geoffrey Keating, Dermond O'Connor(1841)

12) Beautiful Statue like that is made in Cote d'Ivorie, Liberia, Africa. I love the cowrie shells on her head.

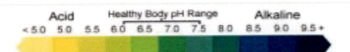

Most Acid	Acid	Lowest Acid	FOOD CATEGORY	Lowest Alkaline	Alkaline	Most Alkaline
NutraSweet, Equal, Aspartame, Sweet 'N Low	White Sugar, Brown Sugar	Processed Honey, Molasses	SWEETENERS	Raw Honey, Raw Sugar	Maple Syrup, Rice Syrup	Stevia
Blueberries, Cranberries, Prunes	Sour Cherries, Rhubarb	Plums, Processed Fruit Juices	FRUITS	Oranges, Bananas, Cherries, Pineapple, Peaches, Avocados	Dates, Figs, Melons, Grapes, Papaya, Kiwi, Berries, Apples, Pears, Raisins	Lemons, Watermelon, Limes, Grapefruit, Mangoes, Papayas
Chocolate	Potatoes (without skins), Pinto Beans, Navy Beans, Lima Beans	Cooked Spinach, Kidney Beans, String Beans	BEANS VEGETABLES LEGUMES	Carrots, Tomatoes, Fresh Corn, Mushrooms, Cabbage, Peas, Potato Skins, Olives, Soybeans, Tofu	Okra, Squash, Green Beans, Beets, Celery, Lettuce, Zucchini, Sweet Potato, Carob	Asparagus, Onions, Vegetable Juices, Parsley, Raw Spinach, Broccoli, Garlic
Peanuts, Walnuts	Pecans, Cashews	Pumpkin Seeds, Sunflower Seeds	NUTS SEEDS	Chestnuts	Almonds	
		Corn Oil	OILS	Canola Oil	Flax Seed Oil	Olive Oil
Wheat, White Flour, Pastries, Pasta	White Rice, Corn, Buckwheat, Oats, Rye	Sprouted Wheat Bread, Spelt, Brown Rice	GRAINS CEREALS	Amaranth, Millet, Wild Rice, Quinoa		
Beef, Pork, Shellfish	Turkey, Chicken, Lamb	Venison, Cold Water Fish	MEATS			
Cheese, Homogenized Milk, Ice Cream	Raw Milk	Eggs, Butter, Yogurt, Buttermilk, Cottage Cheese	EGGS DAIRY	Soy Cheese, Soy Milk, Goat Milk, Goat Cheese, Whey	Breast Milk	
Beer, Soft Drinks	Coffee	Tea	BEVERAGES	Ginger Tea	Green Tea	Herb Teas, Lemon Water

13) Some foods are alkanized and other acidic! You don't want to eat too much from the Acidic group!

14) The Nubians, Afars, Ethiopians, Djibutians of Lower Egypt, Sudan, Djibuti, Somalia, and Eritria have all been mixed in either with Hindus, pale Turks, and pale Arabs, thus a lot of wavy hair and thin features. Now, that doesn't mean all but a lot have.

Isa ElMahdi: "You can find all these features here in the West."

Ayannah Taylor: "Yes, that is what I said Isa ElMahdi!"

Ayannah Taylor: "And plenty of the ancient Egyptians looked like them as well."

15) The cover of the book named Aken A.D Elbe of Germany, Europe. The word Aken is very similar to Akan (Ghana)'s tribal people. Akan is a Twi word and that goes back to ancient Egyptian word Khant meaning "first or foremost."

> **Rasheed:** "Do you know anything of the etymology of Negus, Naga, Nga, Ngu, Negro, Nigga etc.? Is there a reference to us using the word and it being distorted and made into a negative connotation?
>
> **Ayannah Taylor** Wow, you know Rasheed I see the connection but never really noticed til you said something. Naga are the snake people of Africa and India. Na is for Mother and Ka/Ga people in many Niger/Kordofanian languages of Africa. Negus is also the name for ancient Ethiopian kings with the serpent mother blood and of course the original Latins were from Africa and took the term with them in Latin to Europe.

ANCIENT SUDANESE/EGYPTIAN AKANS OF GHANA

ANCIENT SUDANESE/EGYPTIAN	AKANS OF GHANA
Tutankamun (pharaoh's name)	Tutu Ankomah
Akhenaten (pharaoh's name)	Akenten
Khufu (pharaoh's name)	Akuffo
Nectanebo II (pharaoh's name)	Netaneboo
Wahibre (pharaoh's name)	Adakabre Frimpong, Kwabre, Wanibre
Tjahapimu (pharaoh's name)	Hyehapimu
Osorkon I (pharaoh's name)	Osorkon, Osonokon, Osorokon
Meryre (Queen mother) (Name of pharaoh's mother and pharaoh's wife)	Meyere (my wife)
Iniuia (sister)	Ninua (sister)
Khaemtore (Name of a governor)	Kwame Tore (Ture)
Osorkon I (Pharaoh's name)	Onyakopon (God)
Shosheng I (Pharaoh's name)	Susheng (town), Sunafo
Karomama (Name of pharaoh's mom and pharaoh's wife)	Nkrummah, Adommah, Adomadu
Kamose (Name of pharaoh)	Kamosi, Koo Mosi, Kwakuosi, (Kumasi) a city in Ghana, Africa
Khamerenebty	Kwame Kyerematen
Sahure (Pharaoh's name)	Sahureko, Sahurekohene, Sahene
Titi (Pharaoh's name)	Tutu (king), Akwapim Tutu

Were-Imtes	Weremante, Wereko, Brefo
Pepi I (Pharaoh's name)	Pobi (Name)

ANCIENT SUDANESE/EGYPTIAN	AKANS OF GHANA
Menkaure	Kofi Manukure, Mentuare, Asutuare
Merenre I	Manmre, Mereku, Kyeremeh
Meresankh	Mere Sankah, Kwesi Yankah
Meseehti (Prince)	Mese Nti (name, father, uncle Nti)
Tanis (Sphinx)	Tano (god), Tani
Meseehti (Prince)	Bese, Nti,
Montuhotep II	Montu Hotei, Obotei, Montuhotep
Mutemwiya	Mutemwiya, Nyantakyiwa, Benyinwa
Senenmut	Sene mmu, Senenabe
Hor-Awibra	Ho Awibra, Awiabo, Awifo Aba
Thutmose I	Tutu Mosi
Ahmose	Mame Amosi, Awusi, Kwaku Amusi
Kynebu (tomb)	Kyenebua Kodua (King)
Ahmose Nofretari	Amusi Nofre Tari, Amosi Karikari
Nefertiry	Ntiriwaa, Nafe Tiri, Asotire
Tiaa	Tia, Tiwaa, Atia, John Tia
Egizio	Egiso (Kumasi)
Nile	(Nsua enda) Naeye
Pyramid	Pira me (like a sword)
Taibe (Thebes/area)	Te (a) be, Tebi, Tebiaa, Tebubu

Hasheput	Hashe potoo, Afahye

Nebka	Neboka (angry), Abeka
Hor- Awibra	Awibra ho (thief came)
Buto (pottery factory)	Bu (break) to (form)
wadjha (name)	wagya (father), West Weija
Tyu (Name)	Tu (uproot), Tutu
Tshsh (name)	Hye (burn)
Khasekhemuy (King)	Kwesi Kemu, Akwamu
Hathor (name)	Ato/Atta/ Arthur
Khafre	Kwaa Fre, kofre no, Afigya Kwabre District
Una	Wona (name)
Gjese	Gjasi, Gyesen, Gyasikan, Gyakari
Sanakhte	Sanakete, Sankyene, Sanaahene
Amenhotep	Amenhotei, Kwame Tei, Amenhotep
Sahure	Sawere, Sakraman, Saben, Sahurekohene
Min	Oboming, Mintu, Minti

**

16) Albert Pike a 33rd Degree Mason was born (December 29, 1809–April 2, 1891) was an attorney, Confederate officer and writer. Pike is the only Confederate military officer or figure to be honored with an outdoor statue in Washington, D.C. He is known to have dabbled in the occult arts and served as Chief Convoy of the Creek Native Americans during the Civil War period. Hmm, he negotiated to take their land.

Rasheed: "There is only one Albert Pike street in America. It's in Hot Springs, AR where I'm from. It turns into HWY 20 and ends in

Colorado at Pikes Peak I believe."

Ayannah Taylor Wow, interesting Rasheed. You know how the really, silent people who made things really happen behind the scenes don't have many monuments named after them? He and Sir Francis Bacon, don't have a state, temple, street or anything named after them here in America but formulated modern freemasonry the way it is known today. Things that make you go HMMMM!

Jamar: "He also started the KKK."

Makeresia: "What is the KKK?"

Quique: "The KKK is the Ku Klux Klan." :-)

http://knights-of-the-golden-circle.blogspot.com/2010/05/masonic-albert-pike-kkk-by-ahmed-k-el.html

Knights of the Golden Circle: THE MASONIC ALBERT PIKE & THE K.K.K. BY AHMED K. EL-SHABAZZ

knights-of-the-golden-circle.blogspot.com

Knights of the Golden Circle, Sons of Liberty, Order of American Knights.
http://groups.yahoo.com/group/Knights_of_the_Golden_Circle

Ayannah Taylor: "Thanks Jamar A, Victor M and Quique for the additional info."

Ayannah Taylor: "It means knights of the circle or kuklos (κύκλος)."

Ayannah Taylor: "Wow, excellent article Quique!"

Nebuwah H: "He's responsible for the 33 Masonic degrees right?"

Ayannah Taylor: "I doubt it Nebuwah H. That goes to Sir Francis Bacon in the 16th century."

Nebuwah H: "So what is that new movie about Abraham Lincoln about?"

Sista H: "NOTHING TO LIKE ABOUT THIS CRIMINAL, BUT MUCH TO SHARE...GIVE THANKS"

Ayannah Taylor: "Thanks Adika Bell."

Ayannah Taylor: "I suggest it has to do with bloodlines and the Moorish Montauk Indians, the caves in Kentucky which the founding fathers wanted so badly and King George III did too (due to the ancient Blue People were said to dwell in them). King George was mixed and had blood problems (Rh Negative) and linked to Vlad of Transylvania - Vampire. Read Transylvania Moon by Radu Cinnamar."

Ayannah Taylor: "President Lincoln was mixed but dark skinned family- Melungeons are said to hail from that area - Kentucky too."

Amit Maat: "Victor Muhammad I just learned about the Rothschild's. When I see what I've seen about the connections my jaw dropped...Yes Ayannah Taylor - true indeed!"

Ayannah Taylor: "Thanks Amit Maat."

Ayannah Taylor: "I know it did Amit Maat Khamteye! The mighty Rothschild's control a lot of things that happened from 1700 the century on up to now."

Amit Maat: "Yes, now I overstand the reason why Baa Baa was telling us to do certain things...All we needed to do is do the research and we would get the answers...this stuff is deep...got that DNA explosion!"

Ayannah Taylor Yes I know! He Expanded our DNA and way of Thinking!

Al C: "KKK is 11+11+11= 33 for those that know.
One of my favorite books is "Morals & Dogma" by Ill: Albert Pike(33)."

Mikha'el Mazal: "Great post...better comments...everyone is on point."

Muata Ali S: "Yes the KKK is an off shoot of freemasonry!!"

Ayannah Taylor Thanks brother Al Carter and Mikhael and Muata.

Gerald J: "This is a pic of a very evil man."

17) This man's charisma is just off the charts! Otumfuo Nana Prempeh I, whose original throne name was Kwaku Dua III Asamu (1870 - May 12, 1931) was an Asantehene ruler of the Oyoko Abohyen Dynasty of the Akan state of Ashanti.

He ruled from March 26, 1888 until his death in 1931, and fought a war against the British in 1893. However, the Ashante were defeated in this war and Prempeh I was deposed as the Asantehene of the Ashante people and a British resident was installed by the British colonial authorities in Kumasi. However, the British colonial authorities over extended themselves on the Gold Coast, when, in 1900, Governor Hodgson demanded that the Ashante people turn over the "golden stool," and Asantewaa stepped in and fought against the British! This lady was in her 60's by that time! Phew! Go Yaa Asantewaa.

18) A fresco off the wall of the palace of Knossos, Crete. As you can see many different races lived there. Now, none of the original Moors or Hindus is there! Most Cretans are pale but some do retain their Moorish genes.

This pre-restoration drawing of the Sarcophagus appeared in " Vue d'une des faces du sarcophage" dessin de M. Collignon in La Gazette des Beaux-Arts, 1909.

Mack lol

Ayannah Taylor LOL, at what Barrington **Mack**?

Barrington Mack research the word 'Cretan' because Crete was not a good place to be from

Gina Jones BEAUTIFUL DESIGN. I WISH I WAS LIKE A BORDER ON MY LIVING ROOM OR SOMETHING LIKE THAT TO DECORAATE A ROOM IN MY HOME.

Ayannah Taylor Thanks Gina Jones. Yes it is. Very beautiful designs on those walls at Knossos.

Ayannah Taylor: "Barrington you are talking about all the experiments that occurred there with the Minotaur and gene splicing etc."

19) Moorish/African, Bamileke Crown Chief Tcheuffa Ngassa Georges Mathurin king of Baboate. The Almoravids who had converted to Islaam terrorized a lot of other West African tribes since 1000 A.D. The people either converted or half-way converted apparently Muslim on the outside, but still practice their ancient ancestral (Kushite/Egyptian) rituals.

20) Golden Pendant from Panama, Central America. Who is the Moor on that???

This is taken from Four Letters on American History by Prof Rafinasque to J.H. M'Cullough:

"The Negro features belong rather to the form of the head rather the color since there is in Africa Asian Polynesian, black, brown, yellow, olive, red, coppery and even white Negroes. The American Negroes of Karantha, in Choco, the great leveled plain 900 miles long, and 90 miles wide separating the Andes of South America from the mountains of Panama were black with woolly hair in 1506. They are mentioned by Dantheria and all the early accurate writers. The last 2 writers who had seen these are Stevenson, 20 years travelling through S America and he published his book in London in 1825."

21) A Croatian or Italian Moor king of Europe decked out in his entire beautiful splendor.

| 9 | ⊔ | mer ⟨⟩, nem ⟨ | Mer, a name of Egypt. |

This excerpt was taken from "An Ancient Egyptian Hieroglyphic Dictionary Vol. I" by Sir. E. A. Wallis Budge page 136 shows that Moor or Mer/Mir/Muru is/was a name of ancient Egyptian or Tamareans/Tamoreans/Tamireans. Also, in Kenya today there is a town called Meru and people called the Ameru/Amoru/Amoor. These people migrated out of Africa (Ethiopia, Kenya, Egypt etc.) thousands of years ago and settled into Europe and became their Moorish rulers – (Mero vingians).

22) House of Blackheads, Talinn - Estonia, Europe. The brotherhood traces its origin to a group of foreign merchants who, according to the legend, had participated in the defense of Tallinn during the St. George's Night Uprising between 1343 and 1345 when the indigenous population of Estonia unsuccessfully tried to exterminate all foreigners and eradicate Christianity from Estonia.

The earliest documented mention of the Brotherhood is an agreement with the Tallinn Dominican Monastery from 28 March 1400, which confirms the Blackheads' ownership of all the sacred church vessels that they had deposited in the St. Catherine's Church of the Dominicans. In the same agreement the Blackheads commit themselves to decorating and lighting the altar of St. Mary that the brotherhood had commissioned for the church, and the Dominicans in their turn undertake to hold services in front of this altar to bless the souls of the Blackheads.

On 12 September 1407, the Tallinn City Council ratified the statutes of the Brotherhood, also known as the Great Rights. The statutes of the Brotherhood in Riga, Latvia dates back to 1416.

23) Calima (كلمة) culture - taken from the Ashuric/Syriac Arabic root word Kalama (كلم), meaning "To talk, communicate" is from Columbia, Central America from 205 -250 AD.

24) Yep Moorish/Black Canaanites (Palestinians) on the walls of ancient Egypt, Africa. Note their reddish hair tone and complexion. They have been mixing their seed and there were graftations, experiments (like the Tamhu-created white people) from original Moorish Canaanites to pale Pale s tinians.

The Land of Canaan is also called "Lebanon" meaning "Milky white ." In Aramic/Hebrew Milky white is Labawn (לבן) and in Ashuric/Syriac Arabic laban (لبن). If you go there today, that is what you will predominantly see due to all the mixing and graftation. The lepers and pale people lived in the caves in Northern Lebanon and Turkey area. Turkey (تركي) is from Taraka (ترك) meaning "to be left behind, abstain, refrain from." They were left behind and resorted to barbarism, eating raw meat and uncivilized.

25) The Flag of Corsica was adopted by General of the Nation Pasquale di Paoli in 1755 and was based on a traditional flag used previously.

It portrays a Moor's Head in black wearing a white bandana above his eyes on a white background. Previously, the bandana covered his eyes; Paoli wanted the bandana moved to above the eyes to symbolize the liberation of the Corsican people.

26) The "Dalits or Untouchables" are treated Horribly in India and are renegated to the low ends of society. The worst jobs usually go to them. They usually have to clean sewage, toilets, garbage etc.

27) Dikembe Mutombo is the man! He has poured Millions of Dollars into the Congo to help build hospitals and schools there! Now, that is what I'm talking about!!!

On January 10, 2007, he surpassed Kareem Abdul-Jabbar as the second most prolific shot blocker, in terms of career blocked shots, in NBA history, behind only Hakeem Olajuwon. He is a member of the Luba ethnic group and speaks English, French, Spanish, Portuguese, Tshiluba, Swahili, Lingala and two other Central African varieties. Wow! Go on with your bad (good) self!!!

Queene Afro: "And is he living his personal life as an African? Just wondering."

Ayannah Taylor: "Thanks Yarrow Kushi El."

Ayannah Taylor: "I don't know for sure Queen Afro, but here in America he is known to go back and forth and gives/gave millions to build hospitals and schools for the very poor."

Heal Eye: "He is a great guy in person, we shared the same barber in Atl. and every encounter he had a joke to share."

Schyvonne Black: "I met him on a tour of the pyramids in Tulum and Chitzen Icha, Mexico 12 years ago..He is very nice, super tall, and that voice is very unique. We all climbed the pyramid together that day #cool."

Ayannah Taylor: "Thanks Bridget Long!"

Ayannah Taylor: "Oh my Schyvonne Black! You are so lucky to have met him and with a big heart like he gots! :-)

28) Yes the pale and lighter skinned Egyptians were once second class citizens to the original ones. They had a fit when Nefertiti who was mixed became chief wife too!

Yashar Yash: "No such thing as other Egyptians."

Ayannah Taylor: "Oh Yashar LOL, here you come disturbing the peace. In the Torah/Bible it is mentioned. Let me find the verse. LOL"

Ayannah Taylor: "In Isaiah 19:2 it says: 'And I will set the Egyptians against the Egyptians: and they shall fight every one against his brother, and every one against his neighbour; city against city, and kingdom against kingdom.'"

Ayannah Taylor: "Pale people were Slavs (slaves) for longer that being admitted throughout History."

Farrell K: "OVERSTANDING!!! Na Swt Kng^/\^Hotep~"

29) Wigs in ancient Sudan/Egypt were made out of human, nappy hair, or flax. Rock it naturally or Natural wig like your original hair!!! This particular display is in the Ontario Museum in Ontario, Canada.

 30) Ancient Usir/Usi/Usar/Si (Osiris) emblem found in Spain, Europe which was once a colony of Egypt, Africa.

 31) The Great Walls of Zimbabwe! The archaeologists claim these walls go back to 1100 to 1400 BC. Great Zimbabwe is a ruined city that was once the capital of the Kingdom of Zimbabwe, which existed from approximately 1100 to 1400 during the country's Late Iron Age. The monument, which first began to be constructed in the 11th century and which continued to be built until the 14th century, spanned an area of 722 hectares (1,784 acres) and at its peak could have housed up to 18,000 people. Great Zimbabwe acted as a royal palace for the Zimbabwean monarch and would have been used as the seat of their political power. One of its most prominent features was its walls, some of which were over five metres high and which were constructed without mortar. Eventually the city was largely abandoned and fell into ruin.

Also, don't forget the Anunnaqi used to mine gold in Rhodesia or Southern Africa/Zimbabwe, etc. and these walls the original ones are at least 10,000's of years old.

The shared bird/snake imagery of Egypt and Great Zimbabwe. There is a stele of the sacred falcon of Horus from a temple at Edfu, and on in Zimbabwe walls there is a soapstone bird statue at Great Zimbabwe with the distinctive serpentine chevron pattern below as well.

Also lingam (phallic symbols/dildos) objects were found there like in the Hindu rites. Some of the stone 'fertility objects' excavated from inside the Mumbahuru during the 19th century. Measuring about 10cm, these phallic objects are believed to have been used at Great Zimbabwe to awaken the Kundalini energy - as depicted in the accompanying picture of a male and female yogi.

The modern ruins were first encountered by Europeans in the late 19th century with investigation of the site starting in 1871. The monument caused great controversy amongst the archaeological world, with political pressure being put upon archaeologists by the government of Rhodesia to deny its construction by black peoples. Great Zimbabwe has since been adopted as a national monument by the Zimbabwean government, with the modern state being named after it. The word "Great" distinguishes the site from the many hundreds of small ruins, known as Zimbabwes, spread across the Zimbabwe Highveld. There are 200 such sites in southern Africa, such as Bumbusi in Zimbabwe and Manyikeni in Mozambique, with monumental, mortarless walls and Great Zimbabwe is the largest.

32) The bird was found in the Great Walls of Zimbabwe, Africa. It shared bird/snake imagery of Egypt and Kush. There is a stele of the sacred falcon of Horus from a temple at Edfu, and on in Zimbabwe walls there is a soapstone bird statue at Great Zimbabwe with the distinctive serpentine chevron pattern in the following pic as well.

33) The Zimbabwe Bird (above) is the same as ancient Sudan/Egypt Heru/Horus bird! Horus is in the House!

34) This is Mami Wata from West Africa. Notice the snake. She is a water goddess and worshipped thru out Africa and the Caribbean.

In the South African region this snake goddess was called Mamlambo; in Zimbabwe she is identified with the Zambezi river serpent, Inyaminyami; in West Africa today she is called Mamiwata; in ancient Egypt she was known as Wadjet (one of the various forms taken by the goddess Isis); and in India she is associated with both the Kundalini and Shakti, the consort of Shiva.

Ayannah Taylor: "Aset or Isis was a water goddess and connected to the lakes and tree groves."

35) Another depiction of Mami Wata (Isi/Isis, Ishtar, Diana, Ala etc.). She is from the Caribbean and known as Santa Martha. The snake was not generally evil in Ancient Sudan or Egypt except for Apep/Apophis) and in Judeo/Christianity and Islaam it became evil.

The serpent is a very individualistic animal. It bears both a forked tongue (verbal duality) and a double penis (sexual duality). On the metaphysical level, the serpent represents the dualizing principle, the ability to divide into Two.

The cobra or uraeus is the imniprenst protector of all of Sudan/Egypt. She is called Wadjet, or the Green One (Egyptian w3dyt; also spelled Wadjit, Wedjet, Uadjet or Ua Zit and in Greek, Udjo, Uto, Edjo, and Buto among other names), was originally the ancient local goddess of the city of Dep (Buto), which became part of the city that the Egyptians named Per-Wadjet, House of Wadjet, and the Greeks called Buto (Desouk now),] a city that was an important site in the Predynastic era of Ancient Egypt and the cultural developments of the Paleolithic.

She was said to be the patron and protector of Lower Egypt and upon unification with Upper Egypt, the joint protector and patron of all of Egypt with the "goddess" of Upper Egypt. The image of Wadjet with the sun disk is called the uraeus, and it was the emblem on the crown of the rulers of Lower Egypt. She was also the protector of kings and of women in childbirth.

36) Chevron pattern found on the great Walls of Zimbabwe - the Mumbahuru, meaning "House of the great woman." The Great Woman or Goddess Diety is Isis/Esi/Aset, Diana, Mami Wata, Santa Martha, Shakti and her various names around the world.

Thanks sis Naja Njoku for exposing me to Mami Wata (Isis).

There is a beautiful saying of Aset: "I am all that is, was and will ever be, and no mortal has ever lifted my veil."

The words of Isis inscribed on her temple at Sais, Egypt, Africa.

37) Chevron design on outer wall on Mumbahuru (Great Walls of Zimbabwe) is clearly echoed in this fresco pic of ancient Egyptian fresco. So, again where did they come from??? Originally South/Southern Africa! The oldest cities on Earth found there, the oldest people (gene-wise) and the oldest language as well.

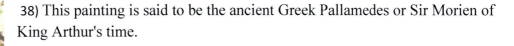

38) This painting is said to be the ancient Greek Pallamedes or Sir Morien of King Arthur's time.

In Greek mythology, Palamedes (Greek Παλαμήδης) was the son of Nauplius and either Clymene or Philyra or Hesione.

He is said to have invented counting, currency, weights and measures, jokes, dice and a forerunner of chess called pessoi, as well as military ranks. Sometimes he is credited with discoveries in the field of wine making and the supplementary letters of the Greek alphabet.

The other Palamedes /pælə'miːdiːz/ (also called Palamede, Palomides /pælə'maɪdiːz/ or some other variant) is a Knight of the Round Table in the Arthurian legend. He is a Saracen (a Moor/Jewish or Muslim) pagan who converts to Christianity later in his life, and his unrequited love for Iseult brings him into frequent conflict with Tristan. Palamedes' father is King Esclabor; his brothers Safir and Segwarides also join the Round Table.

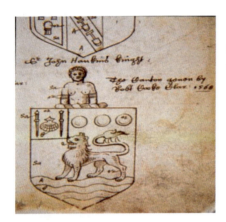

39) Yes this is Sir Hawkins' Coats of Arms! He sold so many slaves and lived amongst the Amers of Nubia, Egypt- Africa for 23 years! I wouldn't be surprised he was a Mixed Englishman/ Mulatto too.

40) Huisheim Coats of Arms, Germany- Europe. This word is the same as Haashem in Aramic/Hebrew, (הָשֵׁם) and Haashim, (هاشم) in Syriac Arabic- meaning "the name."

Hashemites, from the Arabic Hasimi (هاشمي), are said to be the descendants of the ancient Banu Hahsim, or the Clan of Hashim, a large branch of the Quraysh Tribe of Mecca in the Arabian Peninsula. Hashemites trace their origin to Hashim ibn Abd al-Manaf, who died in c.510 AD, more than a century before the advent of Islam. He was reportedly the great grandfather of the Prophet Muhammad.

41) This is the only portrait that I could find of her. No known portraits of her have survived the burning down of the Library of Alexandria. I know she was much darker than this pic.

This ancient Egyptian sister Hypatia, (Hy pasia) was a trailblazer and teacher, mathematician, and inventor of the astrolab and water distiller. She was born in Alexandria, Egypt and moved freely amongst the population.

If she was a pale Greek they didn't have the same rights as the ancient Egyptian women did. Her father was a mathematician named Theon. A Christian mob killed her out of envy and peeled her skin from body and dragged her on the ground for miles then burnt her body!

Joey W: "Damn!"

Ayannah Taylor: "Thnx Joey White! LOL, you are funny! Yeah that is messed Up!"

Gerald J: "This is the sister that the Romans murdered for her speaking the truth about their bull**it story. They killed her with clam shells or should I state that they scraped her body with clam shells till she was dead. . . GREAT POST!"

42) Noble woman portrait after Jens Juel 1775" This is from Copenhagen, Denmark-Europe. Notice how her features are still Moorish but there is much white powder on the face and neck.

Annette G: "The hair and nose are noticeably black/moorish."

Ayannah Taylor: "Yes that is what I said too Annette Garrard! Dr. Edmond Codfried of the Netherlands did most of this research with the paleanization of Moorish European history."

David C: "You can clearly perceive that she is an original Negroid woman unlike some of the false scholars & historians in the analytical group who post Caucasoid, impure images & depictions."

Ayannah Taylor" "Yes I know David C. It is sad how enameling (whitening) of these Moorish/black figures all over Europe has been done intentionally or not."

Amir Tal: "It's really amazing how far the lies go. This why we must devote so much energy to seek the truth. So that we may embody it and become harbingers of it."

Ayannah Taylor Truth and Wisdom spoken Amir Talib El. Amen!

Ray Win: "And tell me that ain't Afrikan hair." :-)

Ayannah Taylor: "Yes Ray Winbush- tightly curled updo!" LOL

Teneerah B: "Yes sis, it is so obvious -Hair, complexion, and features."

43) Pharaoh Natakamani and Pharaohette Amanitore before the deity Apademak found in Kush/Sudan, Africa.

44) Kitaab At Tasriyf), (كتاب التصريف) The Method of Medicine :"," 100 CE by Abu Al Qasim Al Zahrawi Abulcasis - father of modern surgery .He was a Moor/African by race.

 45) This piece is from one of the oldest Chinese dynasties - the Shang dynasty "La tigresse 1300 B.C. found" at Chernushi Museum, Paris, Europe.

Notice the word Shang is very similar to the African god Shango. In the Yorùbá religion, Sàngó (also spelled, Sango or Shango, often known as Xangô or Changó in Latin America and the Caribbean, and also known as Jakuta is perhaps one of the most popular Orisha; also known as the god of fire, lightning and thunder.

Shango is historically a royal ancestor of the Yoruba as he was the third king of the Oyo Kingdom prior to his posthumous deification.

NOTES:

NOTES:

NOTES:

NOTES:

NOTES:

*All * denotes Wikipedia excerpts. Www.wikipedia.org*

** Other Reference books or url's:

References **Akans of Ghana**; *http://lotuspharia.freeyellow.com/id80.html*

http://www.egyptsearch.com/forums/ultimatebb.cgi?ubb=get_topic;f=8;t=006436

Bantu; *http://www.kaa-umati.co.uk/banturosetta.html*

Mer*: The Ancient Egyptian Hieroglyphic Dictionary by Sir E.A. Wallis Budge, pg. 136*

Mami Wata*: http://www.mamiwata.com/mami.htm*

Mumbahur Zimbabwe*: "http://www.humanresonance.org/mumbahuru.html"*

Book of Beginnings by Gerald Massey – **Moor***; pgs. 7, 34, 218;*

Ancient and Modern Britons **Moor** *"pgs.8, 16, 47 etc.*

ABOUT THE AUTHOR

Ayannah M Taylor was born in New York City in 1971. She has been exposed to various cultures and people while living there. This is where she was 1st exposed to the Golden Pharaoh (Tutankhamun) in 1978 while at the museum with her mother. She now lives with her husband and 5 children in Georgia and speaks various languages and has a degree in Arabic and Medical transcription.

Made in the USA
Columbia, SC
28 July 2021